A GOOD DAY FOR DUCKS

Tru +

Published by Ducks Unlimited, Inc.
John A. Tomke, President
D. A. (Don) Young, Executive Vice President
Book design by Michael Todd

ISBN: 1-932052-12-7

Published July 2003

Ducks Unlimited, Inc.

Ducks Unlimited conserves, restores, and manages wetlands and associated habitats for North America's waterfowl. These habitats also benefit other wildlife and people. Since its founding in 1937, DU has raised more than $1.6 billion, which has contributed to the conservation of over 10 million acres of prime wildlife habitat in all fifty states, each of the Canadian provinces, and in key areas of Mexico. In the U.S. alone, DU has helped to conserve over 2 million acres of waterfowl habitat. Some 900 species of wildlife live and flourish on DU projects, including many threatened and endangered species.

Call to Action

The success of Ducks Unlimited hinges upon each member's personal involvement in the conservation of North America's wetlands and waterfowl. You can help Ducks Unlimited meet its conservation goals by volunteering your time, energy, and resources; by participating in our conservation programs; and by encouraging others to do the same. To learn more about how you can make a difference for the ducks, call 1-800-45-DUCKS.

Distributed by:
The Globe Pequot Press
P.O. Box 480
Guilford, CT 06437-0480

Printed in Canada

A GOOD DAY
FOR DUCKS

Doug Truax

Illustrated by
Jack K. Smith

DUCKS
UNLIMITED

Ducks Unlimited, Inc.
Memphis, Tennessee

11103

"**W**hat an AWFUL day," Justin moaned as he looked out the window on the cold, rainy, gray neighborhood. "I'm bored."

"Every day is a good day for something," Justin's mother said. "You just need to find what that is."

"*Urggg*," Justin muttered as he watched the rain drip off the roof onto the front yard.

"Besides, your Grandpa has invited you to go up with him to his duck hunting camp next weekend," Mom added. "That's something to look forward to."

"Your dad was about your age when he made his first visit to duck camp," Grandpa said when he picked Justin up the following weekend.

"I hope I don't disappoint you, Grandpa," Justin said. "I don't know anything about ducks."

Grandpa smiled. "You could never disappoint me . . ." he started to say. Just then Bo, Grandpa's black Labrador retriever, leaned forward from the back seat and gave Justin a big lick on the cheek. " . . . or Bo."

"Well, here it is," Grandpa said proudly, swinging open the door to the little cabin.

Justin looked around the room in amazement. It was so, well, kind of . . . old . . . and small . . . and filled with strange stuff. There was a small stove in one corner and a table with four chairs in the other. At the back of the room there was an old couch and a big stuffed chair. The walls were filled with pictures of ducks and dogs, and the shelves were lined with wooden duck decoys.

"Look, here's one of the duck decoys I carved in my shop," Grandpa said, taking the decoy down from the wall and showing it to Justin. "It floats," Grandpa explained. "We'll put a bunch of these out on the lake to attract the real ducks. It has a cord and an anchor attached to it so that it won't sail away."

"Or fly away," Justin said. "It sure looks like a real duck."

"Tomorrow we'll make sure Bo remembers what to do. Then the next morning, you and I will go hunting on the lake," Grandpa said.

Justin was excited by the thought of going on his first hunt . . . and just a little bit scared.

The next morning, Grandpa, Justin, and Bo went down to the lake.

"Let's see if Bo remembers his lessons from last year," Grandpa said.

"Sit," he told Bo. Then he took a soft rubber duck and threw it way out into the lake.

Bo stared at the rubber duck floating on the water and could barely hold himself back, but he didn't move a muscle. Then Grandpa told Bo to "Fetch" and Bo jumped off the shore, swam to the rubber duck, grabbed it in his mouth, brought it back to Grandpa, and laid it at his feet.

"Now you try it," Grandpa told Justin.

"Sit," Justin told Bo just like Grandpa had done. Then he threw the rubber duck as far as he could, which wasn't quite as far as Grandpa had thrown it.

"Bo, fetch," Justin said. Bo again jumped into the lake and brought the rubber duck back and laid it at Justin's feet.

"Good boy," Justin said, patting Bo on the head proudly. "Gooooood boy."

"When you hunt ducks, you need to hide," Grandpa told Justin. "Wild ducks have very good eyesight and they will stay away if they see us."

Grandpa and Justin cut tall grass and cattails from the edge of the lake and attached them to the side of the little boat Grandpa used for hunting. He told Justin how they would use the boat to take the wooden duck decoys he had made and put them out on the lake. Then they would paddle the boat into the grasses near shore and hide.

"We'll even put on camouflage coats that are made to look like these grasses," Grandpa said. "I've got one just your size."

Justin and Grandpa watched a few ducks flying overhead.

"They are leaving the far north where it is already snowing and getting very cold," Grandpa said. "They are flying south so they can spend the winter where it is warm."

Grandpa explained how ducks follow unseen "highways" in the sky—called "flyways"—on their trips to the south. Then in the spring, when winter is over and the North Country is warming up again, the ducks follow these same flyways back north to build nests and raise their young.

These are the spring and fall migrations of birds, Grandpa explained, and they have been happening for thousands and thousands of years.

"How do they know where they are going?"
Justin asked. "They can't read maps."

Grandpa said no one was absolutely sure how ducks
found their way, but many people think they use their good
eyesight to study the land underneath them. At night they
may use the stars to help them fly in the right direction.

"And some people believe a part of their brains works like
a compass—something we don't quite understand yet,"
Grandpa said.

Grandpa explained how ducks need wet places—like lakes, ponds, and marshes—to find food and raise their families.

"Without ponds and lakes like this one," Grandpa said, "there wouldn't be any place for ducks to live, and no place for them to stop during their trips along the flyways."

Grandpa explained that lots of animals and birds—like deer and herons and songbirds—use wetlands.

"It is our job to make sure these wet places never disappear, that ducks and wild things always have places to live," Grandpa added.

Back inside the cabin, Grandpa told Justin that he needed to learn to talk like a duck.

"Yeah, sure," Justin said, thinking his grandpa was kidding him.

"Really," Grandpa said. "And here's just what you need."

Grandpa handed Justin a round wooden tube about four inches long. It had holes in both ends.

"Blow into it," Grandpa said.

Justin picked it up and blew hard. Nothing happened.

"Try the other end," Grandpa said, smiling.

*Q*uaaaaaaaack came booming out the little tube.

"Wow," Justin said. He blew into it again, this time longer and louder. *Quaaaaaaaaaaaaaaaak.*

Quaaaaaaaaaaaaaaaak.

Bo, who was sleeping in the corner on his soft nest, raised his head to see what the racket was all about.

"Great," Grandpa said. "Now let's get that thing to talk like a duck."

Grandpa explained that the little tube was a duck call. By changing the way you blew into it, you could make different sounds—just like the sounds ducks use to talk to each other.

"Try it like this," Grandpa said, taking the duck call and blowing into it. The sounds that came out sounded just like a duck. "Give it six or seven little blasts like you were saying *Quit . . . quit . . . quit . . . quit . . .*"

Justin took the call back and blew into it the way Grandpa had suggested. Out came *Quaaaak, quack, quack, quack, quack, quack, quack.*

It didn't sound as much like a duck as Grandpa's calling, but Bo's ears perked up.

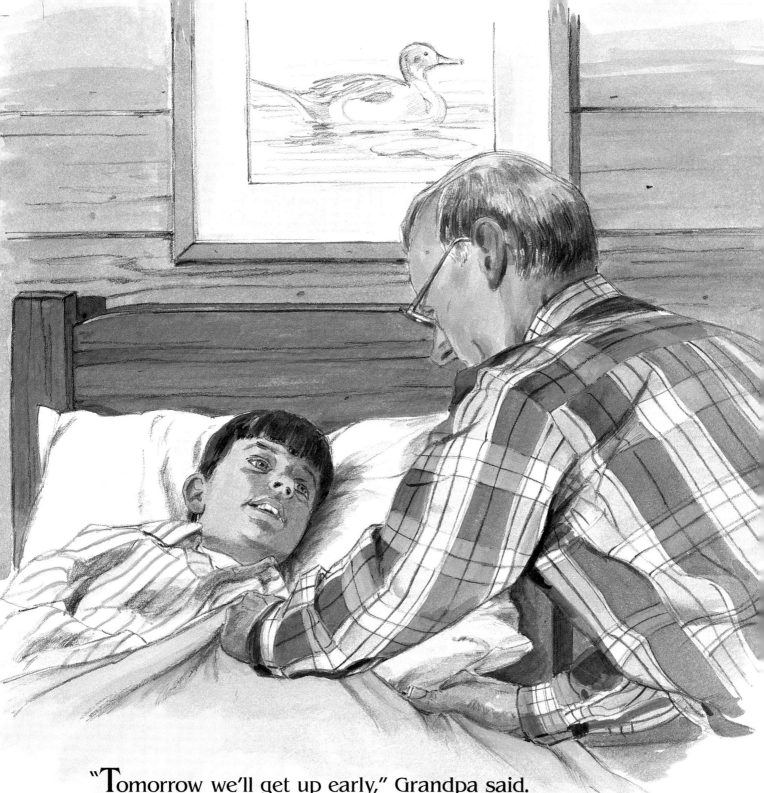

"Tomorrow we'll get up early," Grandpa said.
"Just like the ducks."

"How early?" Justin asked.

"Before sunrise," Grandpa said.

Justin rolled over and tried to fall asleep, but he was too
excited about tomorrow to fall asleep right away.

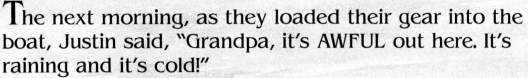

The next morning, as they loaded their gear into the boat, Justin said, "Grandpa, it's AWFUL out here. It's raining and it's cold!"

"A good day for ducks," Grandpa said, smiling. "Ducks love to fly when it's cold and miserable. And that's why we duck hunters love this weather, too."

Grandpa explained that on bright, sunny days, what he called "bluebird days," ducks liked to rest and feed.

"Why do you like hunting so much, Grandpa?" Justin asked as Grandpa paddled the boat and threw out the duck decoys.

"Hmmmm," Grandpa muttered. "Now you're asking the tough questions."

Grandpa thought for a minute as he tossed out more decoys.

"I guess because I love being part of a world that is still wild and natural. I like to watch the sun rise and set over this little lake, to hear the geese honk as they pass by on their way south. I like to slip in and be a part of this world for a little while . . ." And then Grandpa's voice trailed off.

"Here they come," Grandpa whispered. Justin looked up and saw ducks flying high overhead. "Let's give them a little hello," he said as he tooted on the duck call. *Quaaaak, quack, quack, quack . . .*

Every few minutes Grandpa would give another blow on the duck call. "I'm giving them a little sweet talk," he said. *Quaaak, quack, quack . . .* went the call and one duck came flying in toward them.

"Good, now cover your ears," Grandpa said, as he raised his shotgun and fired it into the air. Bo started to quiver and stared out over the lake. "Bo, fetch," Grandpa said, and Bo bounded over the side of the boat and swam out into the lake. A few minutes later he returned with a real duck in his mouth—not a rubber one—and dropped it into Grandpa's hand.

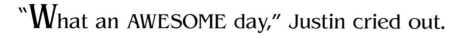

"What an AWESOME day," Justin cried out.

Grandpa laughed as he gathered up the decoys. "It *was* awesome," he said. Then he laid down the bag of decoys and reached in his hunting jacket and pulled out a duck call.

"Here," Grandpa said, "I think you've earned this. It belonged to my dad—your great-grandfather —and I know how proud he'd be of you today."

"When can we come back?" Justin wanted to know. The cabin, which at first seemed odd and small, was quickly becoming his favorite place.

"Well, nearly all the ducks have left the North Country this year," Grandpa said. "But let's come back in the spring with binoculars to watch the ducks raise their little ducklings."

The next week, Justin's mother complained about the weather while they were out shopping.

"I can't believe this rain," she said, nervously grasping the steering wheel. "What an AWFUL day."

Justin quietly unzipped his jacket, reached in, and pulled out the duck call hanging around his neck. He rolled it in his hands and smiled.

"It's a good day for ducks, Mom," Justin said, looking up at the gloomy sky. "It's a *very* good day for ducks."